Broken Lies

SARAA KAMI

Broken Lies

Ahmita Publishing Company
California

Broken Lies is a work of fiction. Names, characters, places and incidents either are the product of the author's imagination or are used fictitiously. Any resemblance to actual persons, living or dead, events, or locales are entirely coincidental.

Copyright © 2017 by Saraa Kami

All rights reserved. No part of this book may be reproduced in any form or by an electronic or mechanical means, including information storage or retrieval systems, without permission in writing from the publisher, except by a reviewer, who may quote brief passages in a review. Scanning, uploading, and electronic distribution of this book or the facilitation of such without the permission of the publisher is prohibited. Please purchase only authorized electronic editions, and do not participate in or encourage electronic piracy of copyrighted materials. Your support of the author's rights is appreciated. Any member of educational institutions wishing to photocopy part of all of the work for classroom use or anthology, should send inquiries to permissions@ahmitapubco.com.

Published simultaneously in Canada
Printed in the United States of America
Published in the United States by Ahmita Publishing Company, California.

LIBRARY OF CONGRESS CATALOGING IN-PUBLICATION DATA

Kami, Saraa, 1968 -
Broken Lies: Poetry/ Saraa Kami
p. cm.
I. Title
ISBN 978-0-9815734-4-1

98765432 Second Printing

www.saraakami.com

Cover photography: Front (Mayer George)

Book design by Dawn Rodgers

CONTENTS
PART I

11	Labor Pains
12	Forbidden Fruit
13	The War at Midnight
14	Russian Roulette
15	The Choice
16	The Bluest Veil
17	Dead Rabbits
18	Los Angeles County
19	Pimps and Hoes
20	Lost Footing
21	The Birth of the Bastard
22	The Girl with Two Names

PART II

25	Tormented Love
26	Silent Screams
27	The War at Midnight II
28	The Choice II
29	The Second Chance
30	What Is Lost
31	2 beds, 1 Bath
32	Sex, Drugs, and Lies

PART III

35	Final Judgment
36	Denial
37	Walls of Glass
38	Revolving Doors
39	Pills and Pot
41	Lost in the Shuffle
42	Piss and Vinegar

PART IV

45	Dinnertime
46	The Sun-Drenched Field
47	The Diversion
48	The Fourteenth of July
49	Messianic Jews
50	The Looking Glass
51	The Courage to Change

PART V

55	The Choice III
56	Doing Better
57	Now
58	Fumbles & Falls
59	Security Clearance
60	Drive-Bys
61	Teachable Moments

PART VI

65	Burying the KING
66	The Sad, Slow Death
67	The Woman with One Name
68	Face-to-Face
69	Selah
71	Broken Lies

Dedication

This book is dedicated to my parents. I am the person that I am today because of your influence. I stand eternally grateful for all of the lessons that I learned from you, and carry forward the amazing baton of courage that you passed on to me.

To my kids, Godwin, Elizabeth-Victoria, Harlan, and Nathan. You have taught me as much as I have tried to teach you, and I hope you will always carry my love in your hearts. I love you so much and thank you for giving me a forever family.

With much love,
SK/mommy

PART I

"Half our mistakes in life arise from feeling where we ought to think, and thinking where we ought to feel."

~ **John Churton Collins**

Labor Pains

He was her King,
The man of her dreams.
He was smart and fair,
Tall as a cedar tree, with beautiful bee-stung lips.
Eyes the shape of almonds,
And a chin both square and soft.

To him she would vow her love,
Accept his ring and take his name.
He was her first . . .
              her Savior . . .
                            her world.
She inhaled his words
Like a junkie ingesting a fix,
Welcoming it into every part of her being,
Swaying under the cloud of its intoxication.

She'd be his perfect Queen,
With kid gloves, bone china, and a white picket fence.
He promised to love her always,
Providing a home to cradle her dreams;
So she allowed herself to trust him,
And every day she told herself how lucky she was
To be loved by so great a King.

It was the mailman who produced the craggy nail
That burst her beautiful bubble,
Baring a letter with barbed edges
Innocently addressed to:
Mr. and Mrs.
Her King had spawned an heir
Bore by another,
And with the news she, too, went into labor,
Incapacitated with each contraction.
She knelt, panted, moaned,
Then yielding to the angry pangs
She bore down and pushed,
Giving birth to the byproduct of his infidelity—a lie.

Forbidden Fruit

Not a hair out of place
Not a crease in her skirt
With the air of a Queen
She reigned in the suburb.

He was from the other side
The place where grit meets dirt
She was the wife of an Officer
With beautiful eyes, irresistible curves.

His caper began on a warm April's eve
Black mask dawned, like a perfect thief
Seduced by drugs and the smell of Brut
Smuggling away the Officer's most coveted prize.

Someone disarmed the alarm that night,
And she slipped out underneath his coat
The perfect wife with the perfect home
Now compromised by his unworthy lust.

The War at Midnight

The Officer's wife stumbles in the dark
Babe in arms, searching for her man
In the alley, behind the country juke joint
She beats on the door and prepares for war.

This time the hand that knocks her down
Is not her thief, but his wife with eyes enraged.
She's not alone when weapons are drawn
Blows laced with venom beget blood spattered walls
As the crowd cheers on the blasphemy
The high and mighty reduced to gutter rat.

Its five after midnight, her baby's cries beckoning
The mother who battles in vain with the wife of a fool.
Police arrive and escort them away
The broken Queen and her damaged babe
Driven to her home behind the beautiful gates
Where her husband waits in the dark and prays.

Russian Roulette

Like a loaded gun with three bullets in its chamber
He spins his weapon, placing it at their temples
Rejection is the bullet that threatens to kill
The loss of his lust—the card rejection deals.

Turning the gun to his wife and then to the Queen,
Fucking with their heads with every empty click,
Laughing and spinning,
While all of his friends shake their heads.
Each woman waits, anxiously,
To see if this click is her end.

And like a thief caught
Red-handed
He promises that
This click
Will be his last.

But this is just the lie he tells them
As he climbs into their beds
To makes love to their bodies,
But never their souls.

The Choice

It was the nastiest,
Cruelest ultimatum,
But the Fool says she must choose—
If his love is to stay
Then the Officer must go,
And the babies *can't* come.

Her babies were her world,
But her man was her god.
His words meant more to her then *their* love;
She'd already made her choice.
So she packed their bags
Handed over her babies,
And paid the ultimate price for his love.

She cried every night as he held her in his arms,
Envisioning her babies sleeping in their beds,
But there was *no* rest for her babies;
Just pain-covered yearnings for a mom long gone.

There are no words to describe
The dastardly deed of making a mother choose
Between her offspring and *her* man,
For there is never a winner in a
Game played to lose.
Just pain and despair,
And a soul left blowing in the wind.

The Bluest Veil

On the day the Officer departed with *their* kids
The heavens fell to earth,
And the sky turned to gray.

He had been the nucleus of her atom,
Rescuing her from a dismal life,
The first to touch her heart;
His love had meant everything to her
And as a reward for his love
She'd given him her blind devotion
And a beautiful family.

Rumors whispered loudly
Among the busiest of bees
Wagging tongues accused the Officer of impropriety,
And the Queen couldn't withstand the sting,
Rumors evolve into truth,
Betrayal replacing a wife's trust.

He said he was sorry,
Promised never again to stray,
But the fairytale had been destroyed
Disdain replaced love and respect
Repaying his betrayal with the card that trumps.

It was the bluest veil
She wore on the day they wed
That now suffocated her soul.

So the Fool saw his opening
And pounced to taste the forbidden fruit
Stealing away the Officer's wife
And kidnapping hope.

Dead Rabbits

The phone resting in her hand,
The Queen lets out a gasp of disbelief.
After months of emptiness, hurt, and despair
The quiet question that was
Is
No longer.

She rubs her belly,
Refuses to tell a soul
Hoping to wish it all away
As she struggles to love her unborn child,
The byproduct of their hollow passion.

Mumbling words akin to the English language
She dances around her confession of sin
Telling the priest of everything,
But the *real* reason that she came
Then, blurting, "The rabbit's dead"
Her Higness now lying prostrate in shame.

Giving her absolution,
He traces her shadow with the sign of the cross,
Leaving the Queen to sit in silence
As she recited her Hail Mary,
and sobbed.

Los Angeles County

They loaded his car on the second of March
Headed west on Route 66
The baby inside of her guiding the pair out of town
Final destination: someplace else.

The Fool's sister invited them to stay
They arrived on Thursday, settled into their room
Then he looked for work on the strip
And for the first time in months
The Queen felt safe.

Palm trees replaced towering oaks
Martinis danced on the grave of sweet tea
Here she was not a homewrecker or broken
She was *his l*ady, his first choice.

Pimps and Hoes

The pimp told the Queen
That he'd make her a deal
If she looked after his girls
Bring 'em clean towels and
Make sure his money was tight
Then he'd return by two a.m.
And cut her a piece of his juicy pie.
The Fool agreed to *his* terms
And every day the Queen
Watched them hoes
And like a Manna from Heaven
Money rained down.

Lost Footing

It all started with a letter in the mail
The Fool's old lady threatened and swore
And like a battered warship limping to shore
They loaded their car to return.

She said she was gonna turn him into the law
For child support he forgot to pay,
Said she'd send out her folk to find them
If he didn't return the same way he came.

So with a heavy heart and a womb fully ripe
The Queen packed her bags and returned
To the place she had tried so hard to forget.

It was a hot July day when they crossed the county line,
Driving in silence, she fought back the tears
Preparing herself for another round of fights
Tranquility now replaced with fear;
Somewhere across the Mojave was lost
The footing newly found.

The Birth of the Bastard

At 9:00 p.m. on the 26th of July
The Queen gave birth to a baby girl
An eight-pound, six-ounce beautiful bastard child.

She looked just like him
He was proud and smiling
Until he caught a glimpse of them,
His wife and her sisters,
Pacing up and down the hospital hallway
Looking for Moses in his basket made of papyrus reeds.

Like the clouds that shrouded Moses from Pharaoh's thugs
His wife and her sisters got confused and lost their way
And the Queen with eyes closed tight ... exhaled.

The Girl with Two Names

It was the most curious of things
More confusing than words could express
How a baby born of two parents
Would bear the name of three.

Like bookends holding together
A collection of first edition masterpieces
Her baby's name was glued together
By the names of her husband and her man.

One served as an act of contrition
The other an act of loyalty
In her confusion she considered everyone
Except her newborn child.

It is a curious thing
More confusing than words can express
How a baby born of two parents
Should bear the name of three.

PART II

"The essence of romantic love is that wonderful beginning, after which sadness and impossibility may become the rule."

~ **Anita Brookner**

Tormented Love

Like rabid animals fighting over food
The Queen and her Fool engaged
In the ugliest of battles
The bittersweet divide of love and war.

They fought over the baby
They fought over money
They fought over his lack of work.

She hated him, but she loved him more
He hated her, blaming her for his bad luck
They loved their baby until diapers had to be bought,
Then she became the moon that eclipsed their earth.

She wanted security that he couldn't provide
He wanted respect that she couldn't contrive
Lust became their prison,
Their baby their ball and chain.

It was a tormented love shared by fools
He wanted more time, money, and luck.
She wanted her old life, husband, and home
Their baby just needed two parents and some love.

Silent Screams

He hit her daily
Beating her head against the wall
Slapping her because the wind shifted from East to West.
Breaking her nose, jaw, and ribs
Heavy makeup covering black eyes and bruises
Blood covered walls and shards of glass the ground.

No more joy in the house on Kentucky Street
No reason to dress up or daydream
Only late-night beatings and primal screams.
For her baby there was no white picket fence
Just hate, hurt,
A living hell.

He let her out daily to work
The job he could never seem to find
Her money was welcomed
Her voice was not.

She no longer cried when he beat her
Her dignity wouldn't allow her to give him her pain
She silently bore the echoes of his rage
Taking every punch,
And planning her escape.

The War at Midnight II

12:03 a.m. when the Queen's sister came by
Saying she'd seen the Fool with another
Hugged-up in a booth at a bar on the edge of town
Not at his new job, like he claimed
Zeus had been caught red-handed,
And Hera was enraged.

The bar was smoky and the Queen was hot
As she stood before her man and his chick
Wondering why she should be so surprised
That the bone she'd stolen
Was now in the mouth of another.

First he was startled, then he was mad
Trying to retain his cool before eyes dancing in the dark
He slipped out of the smoke and slid into the night,
But before the chilly air had its chance to embrace him
The first blow was thrown.

From the left it was the Queen's uppercut
From the right was her sister's sucker punch,
Knocking him cold
And kicking him in the groin,
The Queen landed the final blow.

And in the filthy, cold alley
Lie the Fool
Discarded, bruised and humiliated.
As the sisters stepped over his broken frame
Filed back into the car
And drove off.

The Choice II

What had once been so murky
Was now perfectly clear
Stars now floated on the tides
Sand mounted neatly in the sky.

He had to go,
This point would be argued no more;
The Fool had cost her too much already
It was finally time to shut the door.

There would be no conversation
No words exchanged,
Just the deed
His things stacked neatly on the curb
Locks changed and re-keyed.

No one cried on the night that he left
She wasn't sad,
Just tired,
Broken,
And mad.

The Queen knew that
Tomorrow would never look like yesterday,
From now on there would just be two
And she made her peace with it all
Both the pain and the emptiness.

The Second Chance

It wasn't that she didn't love him
Or that he didn't care
Or that she didn't want him:
He just didn't want their love repaired.

He didn't want her more than all his games
And she didn't want to live a life of lies,
But she still let him return back home
The same day her soul ran away.

Then like a haunted rollercoaster *it* began again
It was love,
        Then war
There was hope,
        Then despair.

It wasn't that she didn't know what to expect
His ways were always the same,
And it wasn't that he didn't know
That her love for him was quickly fading away.

Their second chance wasn't enough
To repair the damage done
He returned home from work on a gray Tuesday
Turned the key and found them gone.

What Is Lost

There was no wedding day with a beautiful gown
No cake with tiers climbing to the sky
The only ring she had was from the Officer
And every time she looked at it
Tears caressed her cheeks
As they raced into the wetness of her mouth
Where they stung.

She had lost everything to win the Fool's love
Gave up her kids, home, and friends
To wear his name that came with black eyes and bruises.

What is lost were all the possibilities of a family
No more dreams of love and good fortune
No more hopes for what could never be.

She took the Bastard
Walking barefoot in the frigid snow
Calling her uncle from a phone booth
And with great sobs
She told him that *their* love was done.

Exchanging crumpled tissues for a set of house keys
Her uncle vowed to keep them close
And within minutes of arriving
The Queen instantly felt at home.

There were nights when the Bastard could hear
Her mother crying herself to sleep
Perhaps she was remembering her babies she gave away
Or all the times he beat her
That caused her heart to weep.

It was the beginning of a new day
For a broken woman and her child
What lay ahead remained uncertain
The only picture in clear focus now
Was what was lost.

2 beds, 1 Bath

It was a red brick house with no garage
With white siding kissing each windowpane
The bedrooms were small, halls narrow and dark.

There were walnut trees in the backyard
Blackberry bushes embedded into the fence
Elderly neighbors looking after the fragile mother and baby
As the Queen regained footing again.

She was happy for the first time in years
Owned her two-bedroom, one-bath house
A gift from an uncle she called Herman.

Sex, Drugs, and Lies

Donna Summers played on the radio
The scent of strange men clinging in the air
The Queen removed her crown and exchanged it for a joint
She was angry as hell and simply didn't care.

Maybe she was angry at God, the Bastard, the Fool, or the moon
But her life took a turn down the darkest of roads
And with her foot fastened to the accelerator
She wasn't slowing down for anyone.
It was the saddest of Greek tragedies,
Marred with opaque rainbows and despair.

There were Black Beauties, Blue Devils, Benzos, Barbs, and Mary Janes;
Then there were the drugs she popped on Tuesdays only, Cartwheels, Chronic, and E&J;
She stayed high to numb the pain she felt when she was low,
Her bastard child was left without a parent at all.

Every month the Bastard was introduced to a new "uncle"
Fat and skinny uncles alike,
All lined the block for their turn on the Queen's magic carpet ride.

She was tired of being tired
Life held no peace, only heartache-coated false hope.
So she sat outside of her soul and witnessed the mangled mess of her life
Now fueled by sex, drugs, and bittersweet lies.

PART III

*"They say that abandonment is a wound that never heals.
I say only that an abandoned child never forgets."*

~ Mario Balotelli

Final Judgment

She was sober for that day in April
Suit, pressed crisply
Makeup flawless
Every hair in place
Standing before the divorce judge
She quietly wept.
The Fool
M.I.A.
Only his lawyer filling his empty shoes
Since they didn't have a pot to piss in
The divorce judgment was easy and quick.
The fireworks that began with a bang
Extinguished without a sound
All tears had dried as she exited the court
Getting her copies of the court order at high noon
By three o'clock the partying had already begun.

Denial

With child support in question
There was no other option for the Fool to take
He said that the child wasn't *his*,
Steering the judge the Officer's way.

He said that she didn't have *his* nose or mouth,
And her hair wasn't kinky enough
Labeling her a bastard
He looked the judge in the eye,
And rested his case.

The Queen refused a DNA test,
And the Fool and his lawyer laughed and walked away.
But sometimes dignity means more than dead presidents
And the Queen remembered to wear her crown
On that muggy November day.

Though the Queen never retold the story
The Bastard would one day grow and come to learn,
And she would love her mother
For bearing the cross of parenthood alone.

Walls of Glass

Secured behind a wall of glass
Was a heart—big and gold,
Hidden away from for the outside world
To protect it from hurt and harm.

The glass made to protect the Queen
Now suffocated the little girl who played alone,
For the wall that kept out the boogeyman
Was the same one that chased away a mother's love.

It is the first prayer that the Bastard uttered in the morning,
And the last prayer that she mumbled at night
Pleading with God to break down the thick walls
That stood between her and her mother's heart.

Revolving Doors

Fake uncles were everywhere
Each one with a vial of snake oil to sell
She was wounded and too numb to see
What the revolving door of lovers was doing to the girl.

Was that door the way the girl controlled the wind and waves?
Could sex one day keep her from getting hurt and played?
Or was it just another way of selling yourself the Brooklyn Bridge
Thinking she could run the show with every man who came and went?

The Queen reigned on her throne and her court was full of fools
All broken, empty, and foolish—takers without a clue
But they brought her pills and pints, they even curtsied on demand
Hoping to get her loaded enough
To end up in her bed.

Her door was a beautiful carousel,
Revolving around and around
With each turn came another uncle and fool
Wasters of destiny and killers of dreams
All of this playing out for the girl to see.

Pills and Pot

Acapulco Gold
Bag Man's Treat
Barbs
Benzos
Black Hollies
Blaze
Blues
Bricks of Blow

Candy
Cartwheels
Columbo Deck
Dime Bag
Dollies
Downers
Dynamie
Eggs
Football
Ganja
Goofballs
Grass
Hard stuff
Hay
Hearts
Herb
Hash

Jellies
Jive
Joint
Kif
Leapers
Lid
Ludes
Mary Jane
Mazzies
Miss Emma
Moggies
Norries
Nuggets
Pakalo
Panama Red
Peanuts
Pinks

Pot
Red Devils
Roach
Roofies
Rope
Rugby Balls
Sinsemilla
Skunk
Smoke
Speed
Thai Sticks
Vallies
Wacky Tobaccky
Yellow Jackets
Weed
Whack

Airhead
Burnout
Druggie
Flying Head
Heavy Burner
Hooked
Hype
Junkie
Monkey Rider
Tripping
Pot Head
Space Cadet
Speed Freak
Strung Out
Stoned
Wasted
Wired
Zombie
Zonked

Mommy

Lost in the Shuffle

It wasn't intentional
But the higher the Queen got,
The lower she sank in despair.

Lost in the shuffle was the girl
Who needed love, attention, and care
When the Queen blacked out
Molestation and neglect gradually replaced daily prayer.

Nighttime seems to last forever
No light, just the memory of such
And a little girl roams aimlessly searching for a home.
Addiction takes many hostages
Leaving victims all along its path
Like the vortex of a killer tornado
With ravenous winds, booming thunder
And a path that destroys.

Piss and Vinegar

Hair neatly coiffed in two high ponytails
With shiny shoes and crisp white socks
Today, she was meeting her half-siblings.
She practiced the perfect smile in the mirror
But their reaction was just the opposite
Full of frowns, snarls, and scowls.

She grabbed their hands
But they stared at her with disapproval, then ran away
Mistaking rejection as a game, the Bastard chased in hot pursuit
Until she tripped on the rug and laughter filled their air.

This scene would replay for the three decades to come
Always the Bastard reaching out for her half-siblings' bitter crumbs
Gallons of piss and vinegar replaced the nectar of a family's sacred love
Leaving a child confused as she searched for a tribe to call her own.
For what she didn't understand was that *their* anger had been misplaced
They were really mad at the *mother* and *father* who ran away.

PART IV

"The day you were born, a ladder was set up to help you escape from this world."

~ Rumi

Dinnertime

Theirs was the tan brick house that sat at the east end of 91st Street
Two cars, four bikes, three hamsters, and a Vespa
With braids that gently kissed her waist
Kimberly was the girl the Bastard always looked like in her dreams.

Filled with a strong heritage of faith and family traditions
The Patton family looked as perfect as their Sunday dinners tasted
With all of their ducks in a row, the family became a second home
For the little girl so desperate for love.

Through Mrs. Patton's influence, the Bastard fell in love with books
Every Saturday, like clockwork,
The Pattons all piled into the family's Grand Waggoner
Headed toward the library for hours of literary free time
The Bastard became part of their fold and soon knew all the librarians by name
As they quickly grew to know hers.

There was prayer at dinnertime at the Patton house
And Bible studies every Wednesday with the Spencers
This surrogate womb was a vast contrast to the girl's real home,
Full of partying, revolving doors, fighting, cop cars, and emptiness.

Even the Queen didn't seem to mind
The world was changing for them both,
And prayers that once seemed ignored
Now manifested in the form of the Pattons
And Jesus speaking peace to the waves
Had somehow provided the Bastard with serenity.

The Sun-Drenched Field

Perhaps it was her way of making peace with her life
Or the way that she anesthetized the pain after the Pattons moved away
But the Bastard would leave home early and return back late
Every day escaping to the empty field where she would read her newest library book
Or write in her purple journal with her fancy pen that wrote in red, blue, black.

She journaled about the crazy things she heard as she lay in her bed at night
All the nasty names her mother and boyfriend spewed
She wrote about the boy she kissed daily
And how she wished she could have gone with Kim
When she moved to Colorado Springs.

This daily ritual gave the girl a sound mind and peace
Taking her seat among the tall grass where she'd sing, write, and daydream.
She was happy to escape her mother's drug-infused haze
And in every daydream she was always light and free.

The reality was she knew that *her* day of escape had not yet come
So she'd wait until the sun and moon changed shifts
Before rejoining the chaos and despair of the Queen's world
Counting the moments until a new day began
When she could return to her sun-drenched field.

Diversions

Donna Summers
Diana Ross
Stevie Wonder
Christopher Cross.

Barry Manilow
Johnny Mathis
Linda Ronstadt
The Jackson Five.

Minnie Rippleton
Neal Sedaca
The Bee Gees
Prince and the Revolution
Olivia Newton John.

Vinyl
Eight Tracks
Cassettes
Transistor Radios
Sony Earphones
Walkman
RCA
Magnavox.

Music in all its forms
Sweet nectar to weary ears
Coping tools to silence fear
Beautiful gifts of diversion
Transforming night into day
God's kindest gesture
To chase the blues away.

The Fourteenth of July

There was no bright, shining light
No booming voice or angelic sightings
There wasn't a call to repentance by an Episcopal priest.
The Bible had little to do with this phenomenon
No missionary knocking on the door
There wasn't a prophet who singled out the young lady
Or a fancy cathedral with all its bells and smells.

Just a weary soul in need of a Savior
Crying out in the pew of an empty church
Asking Jesus to come and save her
To turn her deep misery into joy.

So bending down low, she raised high her little hands
And summoned an invisible God to fill her from within
Then, as if on cue, the anointing of pure love overcame her tiny form
Speaking words of encouragement to her soul and peace to her storm.

Then, rising to her feet, the girl began to weep and sob
And climbing into the lap of her invisible Father, she poured out her heart.
She told him about the Queen, her uncles and the missing Fool
She talked and sobbed and sobbed and talked
Until she could say no more.

For the first time in her life she felt safe
Knowing that God stepped down from His heavenly throne
Took on the cloak of humanity
And gave a broken little girl love, acceptance and a forever home.

Messianic Jews

The Bastard stumbled into a brown building off the highway
Looking for a bookstore; instead she finds much more
Like a scavenger with a treasure map, she explored
Finding surprises and quickly feeling celebrated.

So every day she rose early and joined the members of her new flock
Attending prayer meetings at five a.m., noon, and again at seven p.m.
Soon her old friends didn't recognize her anymore
For her deep sadness had been replaced by the purest form of joy.

Her dysfunctional family was quickly replaced by this new, holy tribe
Who called her beautiful, wanted, chosen, and good
Like a flower placed in warm water, she blossomed under their care
She even changed her name from Bastard to Blessed.

It was in that brown building that she would formerly meet her Savior
Known as Yeshua Hamashiach,
He explained to her the Torah; she soaked in his words and advice
Before long, she'd move out of the Queen's house
And settled into the first *real* home she'd ever known.

The Looking Glass

It was the strangest of realities
A phenomenon too bizarre to perceive
That every time the Blessing tried to pray for her parents
God refocused the prayer back to her own wrongful deeds.

For God was not a psychiatrist
Heaven held no magical couch for her to recline and project shame
He wanted a higher level of existence for her
And that meant not allowing her to live her life in a state of blame
She would have to fight if she was going to win this war
And it had to begin by learning to see her parents the right way.

First the Fool turned into *that* guy
Before long, she'd refer to *him* as "the man"
The Queen became a princess
Then she became human again.

It was biggest act of God's mercy
To allow the girl to see her parents just as *He* did
And to love them with the same cup of unconditional love
That she, herself, drank from each day
For her parents were just human
Making mistakes and living their lives the best they could
He forced her to peer through the looking glass
And see that no one on earth was one-hundred-percent good.

The fallacy that lurks behind self-righteousness
Is the illusion that a human soul can transcend sin
But the truth is that we are all passengers on this journey
Full of goodness, mercy, compassion,
And the capacity to implode from within.

It was the strangest of realities
A phenomenon too bizarre to perceive
That every time the Blessing tried to pray for her parents
God refocused the prayer back to her own wrongful deeds.

The Courage to Change

In fairness to the life she had yet to live
She released the hostages she'd held
                                        . . . captive for years.

Pardoning them all
Through forgiveness
Baptizing them
With her tears.

She released every person
Who'd done her wrong
She released the Queen,
And her father too
She released her step-siblings and the Pattons
She even released herself
For the lies
That she had believed
As truth.

There was a change about to take place
One so monumental that even strangers would buy tickets to see
In the rays of a grand spotlight
Was a blessing, once called a Bastard, who despite her fears
Cut off her own chains
And chose to walk free.

Permission was not needed
No signature of clemency required
She wasn't changing for them
Or for *their* praise
She was simply releasing a bound-up soul
Into the soft, sparkling waves.

PART V

*"Razors pain you; Rivers are damp;
Acid stains you; And drugs cause cramp.
Guns aren't lawful; Nooses give;
Gas smells awful; You might as well live."*

~ **Dorothy Parker**

The Choice III

It wasn't because it was easy,
But the Blessing knew that the negativity had to end.
She started from "I do,"
Choosing a man who was more like God than a fool
She decided to give her kids a life that was better than hers,
With two parents, love, and a faith to sustain.

Like erasing the footprints of her childhood
Every tear and fear she wiped clean.
She calculated a life for her family
That included memories that they wouldn't want to forget:
Birthdays with clowns, balloons, and cupcakes,
Family vacations, lullabies, and sweet dreams.
She gave them life and not death,
And they flourished like wildflowers
Planted on the banks of a stream.

For she knew too much to give her family less
Than the benefit of the pain she'd endured,
And she was determined to do better
Because she knew enough to make that change.

Now her children have a life without rips and tears,
And their children will have a better life still
All because a Bastard decided to become a lady,
And disinherit a legacy of hurt and abuse
That she grew up believing was her destiny.

Doing Better

I am good
I am great
I love myself
In every way
I have value
I'm God's best
Perfectly created by love
I have a purpose
I have gifts
I am special
In so many ways.

These are the words
The Blessing made her children say
Standing in front of the mirror in the morning,
Laying in their beds at the end of each day.
They said these words until they memorized them,
Reciting them in a thousand different ways.

Every day was another opportunity
To plant within their hearts another seed
Injecting them with self-worth and value
Through her carefully chosen words and deeds
The girl never missed a chance to recite this mantra,
Massaging it into their souls to chase their fears away.

Now

In the presence of her children
The Blessing showed up, daily.
Rain, sleet, snow, or storm
Couldn't convince her to leave their side
She'd give them her best,
And fumble her way through becoming for them
The mother that she never had.

If the recital was today,
She would be there today.
If the basketball game was tomorrow,
She'd be there tomorrow.
If their hearts were broken by betrayal
She would stand in that hallowed moment
Broken by betrayal also.

She would give them nurturing . . . now
She would encourage and cheer them . . . now
She would lead and direct them . . . now
She would protect them . . . now
She would discipline and correct them . . . now
She would love them . . . now.

For there would never be a place where they were that she was not
Never a space in time when they would be without her love.
For what the Queen and the Fool had taught her was the power,
Beauty and urgency of now.
And if her babies lived within the four walls of now
Then *now* would be where she would exist.

Fumbles & Falls

With the greatest intentions,
With her heart in the right place
No matter how much she struggled toward perfection
She blew it almost every day.

There were spankings given to the wrong child
Days when she forgot to just shut up and smile
There was the occasional curse word that slipped in a fit of rage
Times when she hid from her family in the laundry room and cried
Despite her greatest efforts to always get it right
Sometime it seemed that everything she did turned out wrong
But she got up every day trying to score the winning run.

For what she learned that the parenting books never said
Was that parenting was not for the weak at heart
And took great courage, hours of prayer, and tons of faith.

It was a thousand mistakes and a half-a-dozen things you get right,
But with each new day you dust yourself off, fall in step
And keep running toward the finish line.
Then one day when she least expected it, she'd hear her kids
Laughing and dancing in the backyard with their friends
And she'd feel assured that for her many mistakes, fumbles, and falls
Perhaps she hadn't done so badly after all.

With the greatest intentions
With her heart in the right place
No matter how much she struggled toward perfection
She blew it almost every day.

Security Clearance

Knowing it was her duty
The Blessing protected her own
Screening strangers as if for a FBI security clearance
She checked everyone for hidden agendas
Protecting the innocence of her babies,
A sacred innocence she had *never* known.

Underneath the cocoon of a mother's love,
Her babies would know a world so distant
From the one of her childhood.
There would be no rapes or molestation;
Domestic violence and emotional abandonment
Would not cross the threshold of her home.

Her kids would have pony rides, exotic vacations
And hot dogs by the campfire.
They would read of horror in the news,
But never experience it firsthand.
She was determined not to allow the boogieman
Anywhere near her nest;
She hovered lower than an Apache helicopter
To protect her sheep from the wolves.

For their peace, love, and joy
She would have sacrificed her very life.
It was her gift to them,
And her gift to herself.
To make their future better than her past,
Giving them memories, traditions and a childhood
Worth relishing,
And a heart-shaped vault to preserve their hopes and dreams.

Drive-Bys

Every Sunday at a half-past two
The Blessing would pull her car into their driveway.
First, she would stop by the palace,
Then she would head to her dad's place,
Car doors flying open,
The sound of little feet running,
Pounding so thunderously that the tunes of the radio
Echoed to the rhythm of their steps.

Fading into the background
She watched her babies
Leap into the arms of the Queen
and then those of her dad.
Like a bucket of waves kissing the shore
Her babies embedded their hearts into the souls of her parents,
And although she never stayed with them
She never denied her parents an opportunity to bond with her kids.

Keeping that bond safe and secure
Became her biggest mission in life,
And her parents knew there was no competition
For their place in the lives of her babies.
They were the galaxy that her kids' constellation hung within,
And they were there for dance recitals, basketball games,
Birthday parties and First Communions throughout the years.

Removing the walls that even words of forgiveness
Had failed to lay bare,
Her drive-bys were as much for her as they were for her babies,
And with every hug and kiss shared between her parents and her kids
She healed
And even though this secondhand love
Couldn't erase the damage of her past
It sanded down the jagged edges of her heart,
Revealing a new layer of tenderness and innocence
She hadn't known was there.
But, this was something that she *had* to give her babies,
The love of their grandparents
For to the girl, to do anything less, wound *never* do.

Teachable Moments

Every time the student was ready
Like magic
The teacher would appear.

Sometimes the lessons came on
The heels of a tragedy
Or at the hands of life's misfortunes.

Disguised as humility and compassion
The teachable moments always
Seemed to come in pairs.

Like the year the Blessing lost her twin sons
And the family rabbit ran away
In the same week.

Both tugged at the heart
Both changed her life in
Different, little ways.

The Blessing was smart enough to know
That her biggest teacher in life
Was time.

With every stroke of the clock
She grew in both wisdom and patience
As if reinventing herself
With every sunset
The Blessing was always better
The day that followed than she
Was the day before
For this she felt blessed
And unapologetically mature.

She was determined to grow
Into the best version of herself
And with every life lesson she mastered
She was renewed.

PART VI

"*Unconditional love really exists in each of us. It is part of
our deep inner being. It is not so much an active emotion
as a state of being. It's not 'I love you' for this
or that reason, not 'I love you if you love me.'
It's love for no reason, love without an object.*"

~ **Ram Dass**

Burying the King

"Amazing Grace" sounded in the stereo of her mind
As she laid him to rest
Saying good-bye to him, good-bye to them.

For the Blessing it was harder than she had imagined
A daughter saying good-bye to her father
Her teacher
Her King.

Time was no respecter of her plans
Providence had to be obeyed
Even when she could not comprehend its rationale.

She wasn't ready to bury her father
She couldn't imagine walking away
Leaving him behind . . .
She wanted to give him roses
While he was alive
Not float them onto of a heap of dirt
In remembrance of him.

But there she was
Faced with this ugly truth
That no matter how hard it seemed
Life required us all
To set a loved one free.

The Sad, Slow Death

The Queen had been distant,
Growing colder and colder with each day
She hadn't ruled her Kingdom
In the way that she was destined or dreamed
And for this reason everyone around her
Especially the Blessing and her siblings
Had to pay.

They paid on the days when she was sad
When she was angry and bitter
Mean words spewed forth with hurricane-strength winds
Nothing for the dying Queen was ever good enough,
And for the Blessing, this made her Mother's death
A slow and painful thing to behold.

Perhaps the saddest part for the Blessing was the fact
That the Queen never fully regained her footing
Born to rule and reign over a Kingdom,
But the lies she told herself
Restricted the Queen from her own throne.

The Queen succumbed
Long before the actual event ever took place
Like an ice crystal trapped beyond the grasp of the sea.
The Queen's final years were shrouded with possibilities—
Possibilities that she never realized.

In the end
It would be an overdose of regret
That would poison the heart of the Queen
And cause her soul to fade.

It was a slow, sad good-bye
For a beautiful Queen
Who spent her life painfully remembering
What the rest of the world
Had already forgot.

The Woman with One Name

Born out of the passion
That united two wicks
From one tiny spark
Burning like a mighty inferno
At the end, only
Beautiful ashes remained.

All throughout her story
She would stumble and fall
Then fall and stumble
Emerging from those beautiful ashes
Like the Phoenix she was born to become
She wouldn't be defined
By the sear of the flames
Or the smell of smoke
She was bigger than them both.

There wasn't a big celebration
Not a parade or firework display
No one called the media
To publicly declare the sacred day
But the day *was* sacred
And magical too
For the once rejected child
Found her way to joy and inner peace
Leaving behind the sting
Of a life filled with disappointment
And the shame of *their* affair.

She would no longer answer
To any other name
But the name that love had given her—
She was no longer a Bastard,
Mistake, accident
Or a girl.
No, today, she was a woman
With one beautiful name—Blessed.

Face-to-Face

For every candle that now burned
Brightly before her
There was a lesson
She had learned.

She had grown from a mistake
Into a lady
And stood today
As the only remaining evidence
Of a sordid affair between
A Queen and her Fool.

She no longer wept
When she considered her childhood
She also no longer grieved
Over being denied her family's acceptance and love.

Today, the girl didn't look
At her reflection in the mirror and strain to place
The tormented soul that she had become all too comfortable
With in times past.

She now possessed something much sweeter
Than the prison that her half-siblings had built for her
Surrounding her now was freedom
Love, self-respect, and an inert sense of acceptance
Illuminating from her soul's holy place—
Buried deep within
Her outside now matched her inside
Both shining brightly.

Face-to-face she stood with a full knowledge
Of the limitations of her past,
And the possibilities of her future.
And somewhere in the middle
Was a strong, beautiful woman
Who was wise and free
And finally, there was peace.

Selah

It was with a heart filled with gratitude
That the woman who was born a Bastard
Stood over her parents' graves
And professed to them her undying love.

For whatever mistakes they had made
They had given her life
And now as a parent herself
She knew, first-hand, what an incredible gap
There was between intention and realization.

Her parents had done their best
All that they knew how to do
With knowledge that was limited
And their own childhoods
That had been filled with disappointment
And much sorrow.

She knew without question
That they were just two people
Whose spark of passion
Never quite matured into a flame
Two halves that never
Fully formed into a whole,
But beloved children of God
They were—nonetheless.

Today, she understood their journeys
And exonerated them from every mistake.
It was no longer about blame
But acceptance
And she accepted it all—the good *and* the bad.

For she knew with absolute certainty
That from the same cup she now drank
Her kids would one day partake
And if not freely given to her parents

Mercy was certain not to prevail for herself
So for her own sake
She chose to extend to her parents
The same level of grace
That she hoped to one day receive
On that solemn day when
Her children stood over *her* grave
With hearts filled with love
And gratitude . . .
     Selah.

Broken Lies
(a.k.a. Yom Kippur)

For the sin which we have committed before You by casting off the yoke of Heaven.
And for the sin which we have committed before You in passing judgment.
>Laying prostate beneath
>The fountain filled with the blood
>Of the slain lamb,
>She was cleansed

For all these, God of pardon, pardon us, forgive us, atone for us.

For the sin which we have committed before You by scheming against a fellowman.
And for the sin which we have committed before You by a begrudging eye.
>Like scales, disheveled,
>Resting in heaps upon the floor,
>Were her transgressions and grievances
>Of the past

For all these, God of pardon, pardon us, forgive us, atone for us.

For the sin which we have committed before You by frivolity.
And for the sin which we have committed before You by obduracy.
>Wiped clean by the same God who would expect
>Her to repeat this same act of mercy
>By forgiving the damning debts of those
>Who had hurt her in the past.

For all these, God of pardon, pardon us, forgive us, atone for us.

For the sin which we have committed before You by disrespect for parents and teachers.
And for the sin which we have committed before You intentionally or unintentionally.
>She forgave the Queen
>For bringing her into a world with such
>Scary, jagged edges.
>She forgave the Fool
>For denying her of the innocence
>Of a beautiful childhood

For all these, God of pardon, pardon us, forgive us, atone for us.

For the sin which we have committed before You with the evil inclination.
And for the sin which we have committed before You knowingly or unknowingly.
>She forgave her half-siblings
>For holding her accountable
>For the actions of their parents

For all these, God of pardon, pardon us, forgive us, atone for us.

For the sin which we have committed before You inadvertently.
And for the sin which we have committed before You with an utterance of the lips.
>She forgave herself
>For allowing an unspoken lie
>To determine her self-worth
>She also forgave God for giving her
>A journey that was both craggy
>And painful to endure

For all these, God of pardon, pardon us, forgive us, atone for us.

For the sin which we have committed before You under duress or willingly.
And for the sin which we have committed before You by hard-heartedness.
>And she forgave the day
>When she entered into a binding contract
>With *that lie* and
>Agreed to the limitations
>Of its terms,
>Especially the clause that mandated that
>She hate herself for the choices
>And sins of her parents.

For all these, God of pardon, pardon us, forgive us, atone for us.

For You are the Pardoner of Israel and the Forgiver of the tribes of Yeshurun in every generation, and aside from You we have no King who forgives and pardons.

ABOUT THE AUTHOR

Saraa Kami's works celebrate the human spirit, the power of resiliency, and personal transformation. She is the author of *What the Children Know* and *When Two Colors Make Three*.

Currently calling Southern California home, Kami spends her life enjoying her two passions - documentary filmmaking and writing. *Broken Lies* is her second narrative poetry novel.

www.ingramcontent.com/pod-product-compliance
Lightning Source LLC
Chambersburg PA
CBHW060518300426
44112CB00017B/2726